Ann Marie Kappel, MBA, Ph.D

Empower "U"

Ann Marie Kappel, MBA, Ph.D

EMPOWER

"U"

EMPOWER "U"

ANN MARIE KAPPEL, MBA, Ph.D

Ann Marie Kappel, MBA, Ph.D

EMPOWER "U"

Build Your Self-Worth
and Know Your Net-Worth

Unless otherwise indicated all scriptural quotations are taken from the King James Version of the Bible.

Empower "U"
Copyright © 2015
Ann Marie Kappel, MBA, Ph.D

Printed in the United States of America

Library of Congress – Catalogued in Publication Data

ISBN 13: 978-0692578636
ISBN 10: 0692578633

Published by:
Jabez Books Writers' Agency
(A Division of Clark's Consultant Group)
www.clarksconsultantgroup.com

Jabez Books

1. Self-esteem 2. Personal Development 3. Self-Discovery

Praise For Empower "U"

Dr. Ann Kappel is a lady on the move! She is dedicated to excellence and committed to helping people around the world to change their lives! This book will help you grow and go to the next level!

--Dr. Willie Jolley
- Best Selling Author of A Setback Is A Setup For A Comeback and An Attitude of Excellence and Host of the #1 Motivational Radio Show in

It's Never Been Done BEFORE and Dr. K has done it! She has woven together the value of having both self-worth and net worth to make and see significant life changes. When a person is on a journey to understand their life purpose and pursue their dreams, both self-worth and net worth must be dealt with. She says, *"Life is so much more valuable than the material things we possess."* Everyone come into this world with unique and priceless gifts which are more valuable than any material possession we own. This book provides simple steps to creating a mindset shift: **think positively, build your confidence, increase your self-worth** and start your journey to increasing your net worth. Anyone that reads this book will experience an immediate shift in their thought life and begin to understand the power of thoughts and words. *Embrace the Journey and Take Your Freedom to a Whole New Level!*

-Cindy Horton, MBA
Success Strategist, Alpha Consulting and Empowerment, Frisco, TX

Not only am I inspired, encouraged and empowered; I am also excited about moving forward in life. As a young professional woman; I was inspired on so many levels after reading **EMPOWER "U"**. This book is a MUST READ!

> *--AO2 Andrea M. Husbands*
> *(AW/SW) United States Navy*
> *America!*

Empowered!!! After reading this inspiring book, I feel empowered to be the best I can be. "Empower U, Build *your Self- Worth and Know your Net-Worth*" is an easy read. Whether you hold a PhD or attained a High School education you can relate and will appreciate the recommendations. This book has allowed me to experience a shift in my mindset, and brought about changes in regards to how I see myself. I am able to not only recognize but appreciate the value of self - acceptance, self- worth and gratitude. Men and women can positively benefit from the brilliance of Dr. Kappel's coaching since the topics covered are relevant and anyone can apply them to live a more empowered and fulfilling life.

*-- **Marlene Andrews***
Assistant Marshal
Office of the Parliament Trinidad and Tobago

This book is a quick read of essential power-energizer tools and pick up lines to line your bare spiritual cupboards in your daily lives. Four years ago I met Dr. K and we became instant friends and cohorts, she was determined to have some hard copy evidence of her thoughts on emotional intelligence on a holistic level to strengthen and uplift women specifically. But... the book is far more than being gender specific... it speaks to any human being who's searching to enhance his/her self-worth or need to know his/her net-worth. One of the passages that got me really churning on my thoughts was the one that referred to the differences in the meaning of worth.

Net –Worth = Assets minus Liabilities – Net-Worth

is what is owned minus what is owed.

Self-Worth – the opinion you have about yourself

and the value you place on yourself.

Dr. K recommends that "you can have an exceptionally high self-worth that is not tied to your possession or net-worth." What's more, you can do it now as you read and hold on to the reflective portions or affirmations in each chapter.

Today as she pens this inspirational book, it is simply the voice of empowerment that is speaking through her. She's definitely walking the talk and invites you to walk with her. Read it and be a part of the movement! It's all about the motivation to have

and to be – *someone of GREATEST worth.*

- - Dr. Camille Brassfield

Maintain a positive, loving and happy attitude

regardless of what is happening in your life. When you

operate from a place of love, the more love energy you

give off, the more love will come back to you. Treat

other people the way you would like to be treated.

Make it a habit to set an intention, each day, to have a

positive outlook on life and be in a place of allowing.

You are responsible for your own happiness, because

being happy is a very personal thing, it is all about you and no one else, it is an inside job. You have a choice so choose to be Happy NOW!

- - Dr. Ann M. Kappel (Dr. K)
Your Emotional Wellness doctor

In reading this book I've realized that you can have everything you want in life. However, it takes timing, the right heart, the right actions, the right passion and a willingness to risk it all. If it is not yours, it is because you really didn't want it, need it or God prevented it.

- - Dwayne R. Husbands
CEO, Wealth Strategies
Brooklyn, NY

EMPOWER "U" is a must read!!! After reading this book I felt energized, like I can go out and conquer the world. Dr.Kappel empowers women to know their self-worth and to love themselves FIRST. Everyone should get a copy of this book because after reading there will definitely be a change in your life for the better....

*- - **Leslie- Ann Walker***
Brooklyn, NY

Dedication

This book is dedicated first to my Lord and Savior Jesus who is the head of my life. To my deceased mother Sylvia Collins who taught me how to be an empowered woman by watching her overcome obstacles. I admired her strength and unyielding tenacity. To my deceased father Simeon Collins, he was the wind beneath my wings. He taught me how to spread my wings and soar high like the eagle. They were my biggest fans and for this I say, "Thank you." I will forever love you both and be grateful for the guidance, love and support you have given to me. Thanks for teaching me how to spread my wings and soar and believe that there was nothing I could not accomplish. To my husband Paul, my children

Dwayne and Melissa, my grand-children Elijah, Myah,

Morgan and Madison and all my siblings; you are my

WHY! Thank you for your love and support and for

inspiring me to persevere.

Foreword

Motivation is key in the process of achieving goals. It is easy to define a goal, and sometimes easy to design a strategic plan, but maintaining ourselves by being focused and motivated is a challenging process. In my experience; this is the main reason why people work with a professional certified coach. A qualified coach facilitates the process of accountability and continuity of the process.

But, most importantly is how can a person remain self-motivated? How can a person keep their eyes on the goal without losing focus? How can a person find the strength day after day to walk the extra mile to achieve the goal?

The good news is that Dr. Ann Marie Kappel facilitated with her book the process of keeping yourself focused and motivated. In this book, you will find tools to develop a strong sense of Self-Worth, and as a bonus knowing your Net-Worth.

Remember, the only person who could achieve your goals is YOU! You know yourself, you understand yourself, and only you know the answer to the question - what are you willing to do to achieve your goals?

Live in a state of self-awareness, allow yourself to live, feel and enjoy the present moment. Open your heart and mind to the knowledge in the universe, and absorb the energy in this book. Take responsibility for your destiny, be honest about your reality, commit to excellence, create your reality, share the energy, define your boundaries, walk with integrity and act with determination.

> – *Wanda Bonet-Gascot, Ph.D.*
> **DrW,** your holistic doctor.

> It's all about energy!!

Acknowledgements

For my husband Paul.

Thank you babe, for being patient and understanding, giving me the space to follow my dreams, and believing in me as I worked on this project. I love you and I am truly grateful to have you in my life!

For Cindy Horton.

You graciously gave this project an extra set of eyes, and the manuscript a final rinse. Thank you for being my accountability partner!

For Angela Baumbach.

You did such an excellent job completing the first round editing and proofing of my manuscript. Thank you!

For my Son Dwayne and Daughter Melissa.

Thank you for your love, unwavering support and encouragement through the process.

For Deaconess Jacqueline Cornwall.

My prayer partner and special friend who kept me covered in prayer through the process. Thank you!

Table of Contents

PROLOGUE

Are You Motivated to Win?

"Your life today is the result of your attitudes and choices in the past. Your life tomorrow will be the result of your attitudes and the choice you make today."

Author unknown

D id you know that your life is created by your thoughts? So if you are not happy with your life, then you need to change your thoughts. The truth: your past thoughts have created the "world" you presently occupy. Another way of saying this is that your reality in the **now** was formed from your reality in the **past.**

You see, life doesn't just happen to you, you have to embrace life or the hand that has been dealt to you. But know for a surety, whether you embrace it or not, the outcome of these moments will create your future "world" by the thoughts that are generated out of these experiences. If by chance you embrace the wrong thought about the experience or process it incorrectly, then your brain will create a chemical that will cause a negative response within your mind and body that will create a dysfunctional "world" for you. However, if you embrace the experience from a positive mindset, then your mind and body will respond in a more positive manner. It is not about the type of experience we encounter; it is more about how we respond and how we think about a situation.

As you become more sensitive to the way you feel or think, it becomes easier to change your thoughts and begin creating a more positive mindset.

When positive emotions are attached to your thoughts, you will manifest more good things in your life. Therefore, it is very important to think positive thoughts, especially if you are not feeling good about yourself because what you think about expands. In other words, this is called self-fulling prophecy. When you focus on something long enough whether negative or positive, you will get what you focus on. This is why you must allow yourself to be in a state of self-awareness because it is important to monitor your thoughts.

If you believe things will not work out for you, it just might not. Whatever you are constantly thinking about and focusing on most of the time, you will receive. It is said everything is created twice; first in thought, then in form. So it behooves you to watch your thoughts as they will take form and become things. In the words of Henry Ford, the business man who created automobiles, *"If you think you can or you can't you are right."*

Self-worth is also attached to how you think. So if you have low or high self-esteem, it is in direct parallel with how you think. Of course, having high self-esteem is normally not a problem, but on the other hand, when we have low self-esteem that is when we need to work on our self-worth.

One of the ways to increase your self-worth is by applying positive thinking. When you feel good about yourself, you are excited to get out of bed in the morning; your disposition is happy, you laugh often and enjoy doing what you love.

Or are you the living dead? Is your life on hold until the kids grow up, until you find your soul mate, until you become debt free, until you find the right job, or until you have accumulated a certain amount of money!?!

What is the **THING** that is stopping you from living your best life now? Whatever it is, let me encourage you to abandon it today and go within and find that thing and releases it. Set yourself free to be happy and to live again knowing you are good enough.

The only person who can make you happy is YOU. I challenge you to take back your power, reclaim your individuality, and begin living life on purpose, as well as being unapologetically who you were created to be.

Also, stop wasting your energy by holding onto grudges, harboring resentment and un-forgiveness. Rid your life of these negative emotions and move forward with life, and be happy now!

If you are single or love has grown cold in your marriage, I encourage you to relive the happy moments in your mind, and then bring them back to life.

Begin performing at your best. When you are performing at your best, from your higher self, you will feel happier, inspired, and exuberant. You will also have a great desire to give to others as well as feel connected.

You will be able to focus on your unique genius, and most importantly; you will have high self-worth.

When you are happy; you feel validated and grateful. In order to feel this way, you have to go within and tap into your full potential. You have to be still and meditate, which will allow you to become centered as you go within.

As you practice this posture, this will also lower your stress level and decrease your anxiety. If you are constantly dealing with anxiety, perhaps, doing this type of routine can make anxiety a thing of the past for you. Furthermore, as you become more creative and gain clarity to move forward, you will also be better able to tap into your life's purpose. At this stage in your life, you must be willing to let go of the old and welcome the new. Yes, there will be an internal battle, but keeping the old cannot be an option at this point. You see, your mind, body and soul are primary real estates, therefore, you have to be careful what is housed there. The most important thing you have is *CHOICE*. So choose happiness, joy, peace, bliss, abundance and love.

Women Power

We are at a time in history where a shift is occurring; the rise of feminine power is taking place. What an amazing time to be a woman! So ladies, take back your influence and stand in your power. Lean in and be your authentic self. Become the woman you were born to be and let your voice be heard.

Speak your truth and take back your birth right to live abundantly. I encourage you to begin living your best life now, living in a state of flow where you feel motivated to win.

Winners never quit! Take a seat in the winners' row and continue to be persistent as you move forward to win the game of life.

PART ONE

Building Your Self-Worth

CHAPTER 1

DO YOU

KNOW YOUR

WORTH?

had the opportunity to speak at an event and while I was socializing a woman approached me. During our conversation, I asked her about her profession and she began to tell me. I then said to her, *"That is interesting, and I imagine it must be time-consuming."* I then asked about her fees. She said, *"Oh, I don't charge because I don't believe the school will want to pay my fees. Therefore, I volunteer and work*

> *So many women are afraid to charge what their services are really worth…If you are not charging what you are worth out of fear that no one will be willing to pay your price…Check your self-confidence!*

with the children at no cost." Ladies! Ladies! Ladies! *This should not have been!*

So many people are afraid to charge what their services are really worth. It bothers me to see people who do not understand the value of their self-worth. If you are not charging what you are worth out of fear that no one will be willing to pay your price……*check your self-confidence!*

God has not given us a spirit of fear!

But of POWER, LOVE and a SOUND MIND.

2 Timothy 1:7 (NKJV)

If you are a coach, for example, it must have cost you a certain amount of money to acquire those skills and knowledge. If you are not at the top of your game to be the best you can be for your clients, then your income will *NOT* be in proportion to your knowledge.

The value you offer to your clients *MUST* be way higher than what you are charging. In order to be paid your value, you need to upgrade your system. You need to put a business plan together and hire a coach to assist you with putting the right infrastructure in place for your business.

You must be willing to invest in yourself; you are your biggest asset. This may include branding, marketing, identifying your niche and—most importantly—setting your prices. But be careful that you do not set your prices too low or too high because your pricing can drive you out of the market.

Also, learn how to monetize your service or product, and solicit feedback from your clients and others, and remember to constantly practice your skills; perfect practice makes perfect.

Also, work on becoming a subject matter expert in your field; acquire specialized knowledge and understand that learning is constant. Once you have this foundation set, you should be positioned to confidently stand in your power. You will be paid for your value, because you will know your worth and you will own it.

> *If you are in business to grow your net-worth, having low self- worth will defeat the purpose of building wealth through your business.*

If you are in business to grow your net-worth, having low self-worth will defeat the purpose of building wealth through your business. You have been blessed with the gift of genius and you deserve to be paid for it. Begin living an abundant life doing what you love.

In this society people are great at measuring things that are external. They only compare tangibles that can be measured. It is this perception that others use to determine who is living a more valuable life: what car they drive, the type of home they live in, the quality and price of clothes they wear and the size of their paycheck. It is in our nature—as human beings—to compare ourselves and what we own to that of others.

What have we been doing? Is it that we are keeping up with the Joneses? Well, basically, we have been tying our self-worth to our net-worth. But the fact is these two things are different. Self-worth is about the opinion you have about yourself and net-worth is a business concept to measure financially how much an entity is worth.

Self-worth and net-worth are two distinct things, therefore, we should never compare self-worth to net-worth. However, the unfortunate thing is that people do judge others by what they have. They can be judgmental based on possessions someone has; material things they own—when in reality life is so much more valuable than the material things they possess.

The paycheck an individual earns is basically to

provide for life's necessities. However, it does not define the value of life. Things that are free and are given to us at birth are priceless and can never be replaced, but at times, we can place such little value on them. I am referring to our minds, our souls, and our bodies. Someone can lose a million dollars and earn it back again, but when you lose your mind, it can't be replaced.

NET-WORTH = ASSETS minus LIABILITIES

NET-WORTH = WHAT IS OWNED minus

WHAT IS OWED

SELF-WORTH = THE OPINION YOU HAVE ABOUT

YOURSELF plus THE VALUE YOU PLACE ON YOURSELF.

As stated earlier, the definition of these two words convey two completely different meanings. You see, you can have an exceptionally high self-worth that is not tied to your possessions or your net-worth.

Some people have a very high net-worth, but their self-worth is very low. And for some, the reason they have a high net-worth—for the most part—was to prove to themselves that they can do it. However, since they really don't have a high confidence level, their self-worth is still low.

But people who have a high self-worth are motivated and happy. They are enjoying the journey and feeling good about themselves. These are the people who have a higher probability of achieving an extraordinary net-worth. At this point, it is important to understand that if you have acquired great wealth, and you are not enjoying the journey, you are losing the game. The key is to stop making it feel like work. Love what you do and have fun doing it.

You might have to walk away from some people (those that pose a threat to your self-respect, self-worth or peace of mind), but it is all worth it.

Your time is valuable. You must understand, the world will lead you to believe that you are not worthy. But I am here to let you know that you are a GEM.

Some of you may be a diamond in the rough waiting to be refined or a pearl still in the oyster. I want you to know that you are VALUABLE. God created man and woman in His own image--you are fearfully and wonderfully made--therefore you are set apart and unique.

Take a look in the mirror and tell yourself, "I am God's unique design." You may think you are an ordinary person, but you are designed to do extraordinary things. Just remember you are your own MVP – Most Valuable Person.

"I praise you because I am fearfully and wonderfully made; your works are wonderful, I know that full well."— Psalm 139:14 (NKJV)

"*You can be the*

most beautiful

person in the

world and

everybody sees

light and

rainbows when

they look at you,

but if you

yourself don't

know it, all of

that doesn't even

matter.

Every second that you spend on doubting your worth, every moment that you use to criticize yourself; is a second of your

life wasted, is a

moment of your

life

thrown away. It's

not like you have

*forever, so don't
waste any of your
seconds, don't
throw even one of
your moments
away."*

— C. JoyBell C.

Chapter 2

LEARN TO

ACCEPT YOUR-SELF

You may be surprised at how many people lack the ability to accept themselves for who they are. Many people are able to put on a front so they appear self-confident when they really are not. The good news is even if you are one of these people, you can learn how to accept yourself. If you are suffering from low self-worth and self-confidence, you really do have the ability to turn things around.

I can do all things through Christ who gives me strength.

— Philippians 4:13 (NKJV)

> *Accepting yourself can mean the difference between a life of happiness and a life of sadness.*

Accepting yourself can mean the difference between a life of happiness and a life of sadness. Making this one shift can do this. When you accept yourself, you have a higher probability of accomplishing more in your life. Self-acceptance can be seen as a foundation. After you accept yourself, you can continue to build from there and add on other qualities such as: confidence, tranquility, enthusiasm, drive and happiness.

7 Steps to Self-Acceptance:

There are many methods and tips that you'll encounter on your way to acceptance as you find your own unique way of getting there.

Here are a few I have found to be foundational.

1. **Allow for Mistakes:** Sometimes you may try too hard to be perfect, and this in itself is a mistake. Allow yourself to make mistakes; simply because, you are human. You will make small

mistakes and big mistakes in life, but it is how you bounce back from them that will make all the difference. The most important part is how you apply the lesson learned.

2. **Live in the Present:** The reason you have not accepted yourself could be the fact that you're living your life in the past. Maybe you are unable to forgive yourself for something that has happened or a certain trait that you have. Getting over the past is an important step towards building confidence, self-respect, and hope for the future. Learn to be in the moment. Don't allow your yesterday to keep you from

your tomorrow; yesterday is the past, today is the present (a gift), tomorrow is the future. Take your eyes off your circumstances and yesterdays and focus on your gift.

3. **Avoid Comparing Yourself to Others:** Other people possess different skill sets and life experiences, which might make you envious. In these situations, come to terms with the fact that you don't have what they have. However, on the bright side, there are many things you *do* have and they don't. You must realize that each and every person is unique. Your fingerprint is completely different from anyone else's. Be

grateful for what makes you different from others, as this is part of your own inner beauty! Repeat to yourself, *"I am perfectly designed and I am called for such a time as this."*

4. **Set Realistic and Relevant Goals:** If you don't maintain realistic goals, you are setting yourself up for failure. The truth is you will not even have a chance from the start! So instead, give yourself a reasonable chance to achieve your goals. How can you do this? By setting realistic and manageable goals that you can confidently achieve. Also, ensure that they are relevant. You may have had a goal in mind that no longer

serves you, so relevance is important. Then, focus on where you are going and take baby steps. You might be afraid to do it, but just do it. Pursue your goals!

5. **Be accepting of yourself:**

Sometimes you don't want to accept yourself because of the way you look. Society puts some serious pressure on people that way.

Focus on your positive attributes and overall health.

Remember that people in magazines are usually airbrushed and have to maintain a certain figure; you shouldn't strive to look like them. Instead, focus on your positive attributes and overall health. Remember their perception of you is not your reality. You create your own reality.

Override the negative self-talk by speaking out loud and affirming positive words that will cancel out the negative.

6. Think Positive Thoughts: One of the most important accomplishments on the journey to accepting yourself is learning to think positively. It's easy to forget how much power there is in our thoughts. Remember, whatever you think about expands. Therefore, the more you think positively about yourself, the more accepting you will become of yourself. If you make an effort to think a certain way, you can actually change your manner of thinking, and therefore, change your actions. POSITIVE THINKING LEADS TO POSITIVE ACTIONS. This ultimately leads to feeling good about yourself. Override the negative self-talk by speaking out loud and affirming positive words that will cancel out the negative. Use "POWER WORDS" as you look yourself in the mirror.

If you are hearing the voice in your head saying; "Who do you think you are to start a business? Girl, do you think you will really loose

that weight?" then your power word response

could be something like this:

"I *AM* good enough and there *IS* more

for me to learn."

"There *IS* more than enough for everyone.

"I love myself and I *AM* lovable!"

7. **Help From Your Loved Ones:** Your loved ones

could be of an assistance to you in this stage of

your life. They might be able to help you get

some outside perspective on your problems. We

sometimes tend to be our own worst critic, but

family members can often give us generous support and love. But if the family relationship is toxic, then you must seek others for advice. You will be happier once you have come to this same realization as well.

Hopefully, these strategies have been a blessing to you. And if you take these strategies to heart you will learn to accept yourself. You will find the world is a wonderful place and you will enjoy your place in it!

Self-Love: Self-love is the greatest of all love. If you do not love yourself; it is difficult to open yourself up to love or be loved. You consist of the body, mind, soul and spirit. If all of these areas are not in proper

> *We have the ability to expand our thoughts to create our own map of reality.*

alignment; then your life will be off balance.

This can lead to not feeling good about yourself. Ask yourself, "Who am I?" Wait for an answer... it will come. We form the reality of who we are based on the beliefs we grew up with. It is time to challenge those beliefs. Those beliefs—for the most part—are inherited behaviors and emotions we learned as children. It might seem that we are given a map to live by; something that is already created for us. However, this pattern of self-love might not be your true reality. We have the ability to expand our thoughts to create our own map of reality. People respond to their self-created maps of reality, not to reality set by others.

For example, if obesity runs in your family and you truly believe you will also become obese, then it will be so. Truly, you become what you think about most of the time. Thus, it will serve you to begin thinking good things about yourself. What you believe shapes what you think about yourself. Just as you were provided a map when you were child—by the words you heard—you have been molded and are affected by those words as an adult. The good news is that you can retrain your brain to think differently and ultimately change your life. This will create new words and create a new and real map: Your map.

Get in the habit of repeating daily affirmations about what you want for your life and how you want to be seen by others and yourself. Write them out and repeat several times during the day until it becomes programmed into your brain. Remember to make it real, because your brain believes what it feels.

"Your subconscious mind

will act to the given instructions

that are emotionalized and handed

over to it with feelings."

— Napoleon Hill.

Daily Affirmations:

I am good enough. I approve of and love myself. I am loved: I accept who I am. I expect good things to happen to me. Loving people are always attracted to me. I give myself permission to love me just as I am. Every day in every way I am getting better and better. I am fearfully and wonderfully made in God's image.

Our thoughts are very powerful. You can believe something about yourself and it can come to pass. Yes, your expectation of yourself can change. If you expect great things in your life, then you can have them. What you have to do is open yourself up to opportunities and step outside of your system of belief; *your old ways of thinking.*

Think about what drives you, what motivates you, what makes you want to get out of bed each morning. What do you want and expect out of life?

You see, you have to train yourself to be happy. When you are happy, it improves everything you do. It even affects what you bring into other people's lives. When you build up a reservoir of unshakable faith, you then boost your expectancy. When you believe for something to happen in your life, you place yourself in the state of expectancy. Begin your day by affirming what you are expecting, and then you state your desire. Believe it is possible and then expect that—by faith—you will have it.

Also, one of the most important acts—as you wait in expectancy—is to be in a spirit of gratitude. Each day, get in the habit of appreciating all that you already have. I personally begin my day with prayer, praise and worship, and meditation and visualization. After that, I set my intentions for the type of day I expect to have. I encourage you to get in the habit of "pre-paving" your day as well. List exactly what you desire to see unfold each day. Do it before you begin your day and expect it to happen. You have the ability to change your attitude, your income, living conditions, relationships and your health with your thoughts.

When you begin to change the way you see yourself, you will experience a real change in your life. Ask yourself, *"Do I have a fixed or a growth mindset?"* If you have a fixed mindset that you cannot do a thing, then more than likely you will not be able to do that thing. However, when you have a growth mindset, you

> *If you have a fixed mindset, you believe that you cannot do a thing. When you have a growth mindset, you suddenly begin to change your outlook and positive things begin to happen.*

will have a sudden change in your outlook on life and positive things will begin to happen to you. Remember: POSITIVE THINGS HAPPEN TO POSITIVE PEOPLE.

Do not worry about what might go wrong, but rather fix your thoughts on what might go right. Rise above negativity, negative people, negative environment, and negative thoughts. When you do this, you will find you are growing in areas you had not anticipated. As the old adage goes, YOUR ATTITUDE DETERMINES YOUR ALTITUDE. So feel good about yourself and be grateful for who you are becoming.

Nothing is given to man

on earth – struggle is

built into

the nature of life, and

conflict is possible – the

hero/heroine is the

man/woman who lets no

obstacle prevent him/her

from pursuing the values

he/she has chosen.

— Andrew Bernstein

Chapter 3

BUILDING
SELF-CONFI-
DENCE

I t is said that inside of every woman is a little girl who stands guard at her heart in order to protect it. For some, this little girl has been there for so long that it has become the norm. It is time to go within and find that little girl, so that the little girl might grow up. It's time to tell her that it is safe to come out; it is safe to open up her mind to change and growth. It is time to reactivate dreams that have been deferred as well as aborted. As well, it is time to refresh those dreams that are stuck.

Women are very influential beings, and unfortunately, some women have lost that influence. They have allowed fear to get the best of them and this fear can be crippling. This **F.E.A.R.** is **FALSE EVIDENCE APPEARING REAL**. Many women have experienced situations in their life that were not very pleasant. They were downright hash or even brutal. Some of these events could go as far back as childhood. You may have been raped, abused, mistreated, or molested, and in some instances the perpetrator may have been a relative.

You may feel beaten down by the stressors of life. You may have been told you will not be anything. You are not good enough. I am sorry you were born. You are not pretty. You are not smart. You are not worthy. You are not college material.

Maybe your dad might have been an absentee father. Maybe you grew up in a negative environment, or you just never felt good about yourself. For all those years, that little girl has been protecting your heart. But now is the time to make a decision and tell that little girl, *"It is alright; you can rest. Help is on the way."*

Women, once you release her; you should begin to feel better. There should be a relief. Imagine that little girl saying, "Thank you! Thank you for releasing me!"

Now imagine you saying, *"Thank you! You can rest; you do not need to protect me anymore."*

Now, if you are a woman reading this, let me encourage you to stop right now and take a few deep breath and release it slowly. What I want you to do is breathe in confidence and breathe out insecurity. Breathe in possibility and breathe out hopelessness. Breathe in faith and breathe out fear. From this time forward you can begin living the life of your dreams. Also, start living on purpose, expand your borders, so that you can find freedom. Remember: THE ULTIMATE PRIZE IS JOY AND LOVE.

As you begin to open up your heart; you will experience freedom like never before. THEREFORE,

BOLDLY DECLARE WHO YOU ARE.

In this present moment, allow the God of this Universe in to open up your heart and provide that safe place. A place where you allow love, joy, and laughter to flow freely. Take your freedom to a whole new level; a place that you have never been before.

Affirmation:

I am limitless; I am awesome; I am a unique individual.

I am confident and I love myself.

Building Confidence

A person's posture speaks volume. It is said that women who tend to have slumped shoulders and move slowly about tend to exude a lack of self-confidence. - But I have found out this is the same with men. - They tend to stay in the shadows and consider themselves unimportant. These types of women will also lack positive energy in their lives. When you come in contact with women like this, they have weak handshakes and they seldom make eye contact with you. On the other hand, if women are in the habit of exhibiting good posture, having square shoulders, sitting upright, making good eye contact and having good energy, these types of women have the tendency to feel more empowered and confident.

Habit of a Confident Woman: Power Pose

Some women like the "Wonder Woman Pose"—standing tall with their hands on their hip with their chest out—as it gives them a sense of confidence. We speak with verbal language, but more powerfully, we can speak with our body language: how we sit, how we stand, and our facial expressions. This, literally, can change our physiology and influence how others perceive us. It is so impactful to know that body language effects how others see us, but it is so much more impactful to know what it does to yourself. It absolutely changes HOW YOU FEEL ABOUT YOURSELF.

At Harvard University, Professor Amy Cuddy's research showed that, in addition to changing how you feel, your posture also changes your hormone levels in a meaningful and significant manner. Standing in a power pose for as little as two minutes can boost your confidence because it raises your testosterone levels, changes your mood and lowers your cortisol levels; ultimately reducing anxiety. This is perfect when you have an interview, business negotiation, or speaking engagement. This truly can have an overall shift on your health. The result: **High Power** body language is open and relaxed and **Low Power** body language is closed and guarded.

This is a typical example of renewing your mind and changing your life. The simple act of practicing the "Wonder Woman Pose" two minutes each day—until you begin building your confidence level—can make a

big difference. As you stand, see yourself as the leader that you are. Even if you don't *feel* it initially, continue practicing until it becomes your normal. Get in the habit of acting "as if," until it actually happens. Remember: It first happens in your thoughts.

This can work for both men and women. All it takes is two minutes. For a morning routine stand in your power pose for two minutes, with eyes closed, and visualize your day. See yourself accomplishing all that you have

> *Being confident involves both your mind and body. Therefore, understand that your emotional state will impact your confidence level.*

to do, breathe in deeply for a count of 3, hold for 1, then breathe out fully for a count of 5. This exercise can boost your day; pre-paving it by visualizing, doing the breathing exercises and power posing. All the while, allowing you to have a relaxed, stress-free and confident day.

Being confident involves both your mind and body. Therefore, understand that your emotional state *will* impact your confidence level. Learn to be mindful of your body language and expand your physical presence. Powerful and successful leaders not only think a certain way; they also carry themselves in a certain manner.

Being able to stand up at networking events and give your 30 second commercial can definitely boost your self-confidence. Write an attention grabbing commercial of yourself highlighting your 'WHY.' "Why" describes what you do. Practice it by saying it aloud. Look in the mirror or have a loved one critique you. This will help you to perfect your "why" and make it powerful when you do stand up and deliver it.

I have found this formula to be helpful: "I help people_____ (list what you help them DO) so they can HAVE_____ (list what you help them get)." Fill in the blanks and create your elevator pitch. Go out and speak what you are seeking. Learn to lead from within.

I will give thanks to you, for I am fearfully and

wonderfully made; wonderful are your works

and my soul knows it very well. —Psalm 139:14(ASV)

7 Ways to Raise Your Self-Worth

Having a sense of self-worth and an opinion of yourself without grandiosity is important to be able to live a life of success. Some people need others to validate them. They sometimes base their self-worth on the material things they possess in order to feel good. All that really matter is how you feel about yourself. Once you find it within you to build your self-worth, your life will take a different trajectory.

1. **Do things you Enjoy**: As you spend more time doing things you enjoy; you will begin to feel better about yourself. The brain has the ability to produce a chemical called endorphins, and when released; it increases a good feeling on the inside that causes you to experience joy and a sense of well-being.

2. **Relive Happy moments:** When engaged in activities you enjoy, the brain has the ability to recall the things you love. Once these memories are activated, it can boost your self-esteem as you relive the happy moments.

3. **Journaling:** Form a habit of writing at least three things you appreciate about yourself each day. Also, write about things you love and are grateful for. Give yourself a self-appreciation break. When we feel good about the things we excel at those things help us to feel better about ourselves.

4. **Stop self-sabotaging:** You can be your worst enemy. Raising your vibration about how you feel about yourself causes you to feel more deserving. Say "stop" to your inner critics. Once you begin to love yourself more, then things become easier to handle and you are less likely

to self-sabotage. Surround yourself with positive energy. You may need to change your circle of friends if they are negative talking individuals. Once you begin to love yourself, you become happier, therefore, more "happier" people will be attracted to you and you will be attracted to more "happier" people.

5. **Your Self-Worth should not be measured by Others:** Everyone has their own map of reality. Therefore, you should not allow anyone to determine your self-worth. You can and have the ability to create your own reality. You do not have to seek validation from other people.

Know that others will measure your self-worth based on their deficiencies. Learn to see yourself through your own lens; then you can measure your worth from the inside out. Believe in yourself enough to know, **you are capable of accomplishing and attaining your goals and desires**. Just trust in the process and your ability.

6. **Think Positive Thoughts:** Thoughts become things. Be careful what you are thinking about from moment to moment; being in a state of awareness allows you to monitor your thoughts. All things are made up of energy, since what you

think about expands, then if your thoughts are positive you will attract more positive things. Conversely, if you are thinking negative things you will attract more negative things to yourself. In order to boost your self-esteem keep focusing your thoughts on the things you desire and they will be attracted to you.

7. **Act "As If":** You have to act "as if" you already have what you desire. Faith is the evidence of things that you are hoping for, but you have not yet seen the physical evidence of it. It is the same concept believing you already have it before you get it, acting "as if". You will have to

change your vocabulary. Instead of saying, "I want to live an abundant life," say "I am living a life of abundance," "I am healthy," "I am limitless," "I am good enough."

These simple steps to raise your self-esteem and self-worth are easy to put into your day-to-day practice. Start today to build your self-worth and self-esteem and make it the foundation of your character. Your life will never be the same.

If low self-esteem has you feeling uninspired, there are brighter days ahead. You have the power to renew your ego within a matter of days. You may need to put in a little bit of work to overcome the roadblocks in the way of your rising self-esteem, but your efforts will certainly be worth it.

Tips to Renew your Ego

What are your Needs: Do not allow anyone to deter you from living a life of happiness. Their thoughts about decisions you make are worthless. The most important thing you have is your ability to CHOOSE. Therefore, choose to be happy and do not worry about what others are saying; it is only noise. I encourage you to free your mind, forget about keeping up with appearances and material things only to impress others. Focus on what you desire and the things that will change your vibration and allow you to feel happy. Begin to live life on your terms.

Relinquish the fear of judgment: When you allow yourself to be free from the fear of being judged by others, your situation will begin to change. New opportunities will begin to present themselves to you, things that were once a dream will become alive for you and you will begin to feel good about yourself.

Set boundaries and do not allow negativity to enter into your space. You do not have to keep up with the "Joneses." Occasionally, it will help to get advice from others. However, if it begins to turn into criticism and judgment disassociate yourself from the conversation. We tend to adjust to what others say we can do and clouds our judgment. Never judge your clarity on how other people respond. Create your own reality and do not allow anyone to dictate your life, put yourself first.

Your Image speaks a lot about You: You will immediately boost your ego when you make changes to your image and appearance. When you look in the mirror and you look good, you will ultimately feel good. It is often said the first impression is a lasting impression. Presenting yourself in a manner that is stylish and neat will allow you to walk confident. When others see you for the first time and your appearance is pleasing to the eyes, you will be remembered. If your appearance is causing you to feel bad about yourself, change it.

Taking care of yourself from the inside out is very

important. Exercise often, get sufficient sleep, drink water, eat healthy and laugh often. Take care of your skin and hair daily and take pride in your appearance by ensuring you are dressed to suit the occasions. It does not have to be costly to look good.

Assess your Circle: Who are you surrounding yourself with? Is it people who appreciate and care about your best interest? If theré is a lot of negative energy in your circle of friends and family and you let them know it is negatively impacting your well-being, but nothing changes, you need to distance yourself. Constantly, being in the presence of negativity lowers your self-esteem and brings about unwarranted stress.

Also, if everyone in your circle is constantly pulling from you for advice and motivation because you are the strongest one, your circle is dysfunctional and you need to change it. Sometimes you have to cut, demote and fire people in your circle. Whatever is required to develop a healthy ego and build your self-worth, **do it!** Sometimes it takes removing yourself from the negative energy to spur up your life. You will definitely feel better about raising your level of happiness.

By effectively implementing these tips, you will begin to notice a rise in your self-esteem as you begin to build your self-worth. Remember, *you are worth the effort;* the world is awaiting your contribution**! Do not allow others to silence the greatness that is inside of** you, so learn to live life from your higher self, on your

terms.

Chapter 4

SUCCESS MINDSET

Developing a mindset geared towards success also helps to boost your confidence. In order to change the way you think, you have to create awareness around your emotions. Being aware of how you feel—whether it is anxious, fearful, sad, or hopeless—is very important in changing the way you think. These are all limiting beliefs or emotions. The ability to control your emotions allows you to cultivate a calm demeanor to communicate with confidence.

However, despite the fact that you share this world with others, you do not share the same reality. The manner in which you see the world—and the way you understand it—can be completely different from someone that might be living in your home or; perhaps, someone sitting next to you in a meeting. When you understand and accept that you create your own reality, things begin to shift for you.

Your individual views of the world were formed based on the environment you grew up in; what you saw, heard, were told and experienced. This is the reality you were born into. But you have the ability to change your reality by changing your belief. If you have low self-esteem; you can increase your confidence by shifting your beliefs.

> *Train yourself to become aware of your thoughts and begin functioning from your higher self.*

For many years it was thought that once developed, the human brain was fixed and unable to change. However, scientists have discovered that the brain is malleable. This means that it can change. It is known as Neuroplasticity. It shows that the brain is continuously changing, forming and growing new neurons and connections. Therefore, we really do have the ability to change our brain by the way we think.

Train yourself to become aware of your thoughts and begin functioning from your higher self. When you begin to experience an emotion—whether it is sadness, fear, anxiety or doubt—begin to challenge the thought by thinking happy thoughts. Ask yourself, "Is this a belief or a fact that is triggering the emotion?" If it is a belief, ask yourself, "How is this serving me?" If it is not serving your best interest—which for the most part it is not—think about something that is more empowering.

You have the ability to change it. One way to create new pathways in the brain is by overriding existing beliefs and reinforcing new beliefs. Reciting affirmations using repetition is another way. Here are some more affirmations you can use:

Affirmations:

I am beautiful. I am worth loving. I accept myself. I trust my inner wisdom. I open new possibilities to my life. I give myself permission to release all fear and doubt. I allow myself to accept my uniqueness. I am limitless. I am successful. I am all-knowing and powerful. I am at peace with my age and my body. I stand in my own power and create my own reality.

As you repeat these affirmations; you must add

emotions and feelings to them. Post them in obvious places like your bathroom mirror, your refrigerator, and your desk... even in your purse. Repeat them first thing in the morning, during the day, and the last thing before you go to bed. The more you affirm a thought, the more your mind will accept it.

If during the day you feel your confidence begins to slip or if you begin to waver, look at your affirmations and focus on them for a while. You will need to recharge sometimes during the day. Just as your cellular phone needs to be recharged; you might need a boost in your confidence also.

Take a break, close your door or go to the bathroom and recharge. Whether it is deep breathing, your power pose, or repeating your affirmations, make it a habit to recharge your energy at some point during the day.

When people do not feel good about themselves, they have a propensity to project what they feel upon others.

Speaking negatively about yourself and others can be very toxic and causes you to feel less empowered. Therefore, in order to cultivate good feelings in your life, you must break certain cycles as well. Avoid gossiping, being judgmental, jealous, resentful, disrespectful and rude towards others because the root cause of these behaviors can be based on the beliefs that are buried in your subconscious. These negative thoughts are hidden and can cause you to have low self-esteem.

When people do not feel good about themselves; they have a propensity to project what they feel upon others. So, if you do not feel good about yourself; then you might have more of a tendency to gossip about others. You also might have a tremendous problem paying another woman a compliment. You will speak badly about others when they are absent.

When you develop a positive mindset; you will no longer attract that negative energy. You will be able to compliment others in your presence and speak well of people. You can even learn to bless others when they attain success. You see, once you begin to identify the good in others, it will have an impact on how you feel and it will boost your confidence level as a result. Also, you will build a stronger following of people who enjoy being around you. But let me caution you, you might have to demote and fire friends... *maybe even some relatives that no longer serve your higher self.* If so, be strong and courageous!

Six Signs of Self-doubt?

When you are experiencing self-doubt, you can feel defeated. If you find yourself being pulled into negative thoughts from past experiences, focus on positive thoughts. Conversely, when you begin feeling good about yourself, your self-esteem increases and you are more likely to experience great success in every area of your life. When you are no longer experiencing self-doubt, you will live a happier more fulfilling life; build stronger relationships, and be respected more by others. Anyone who is consistently experiencing self-doubt is living beneath their potential.

1. **Being too Sensitive:** People with a low self-efficacy can be sensitive to criticism; as a result they are extremely defensive. Having low self-confidence causes you to feel insecure, thereby, making it difficult for you to accept who you are. Once you begin to feel better about who you

are, and *whose* you are – a child of the creator of this Universe - you will view criticism as constructive feedback. You are open and receptive to learn ways that will help you to improve.

People who are experiencing self-doubt find it challenging to spend time in silence; therefore, they are frequently wanting to be in the company of others and sometimes even dominating the conversation.

2. **Fear of Being Alone:** Just the fear of being alone can cause people to feel insecure and anxious. People who are experiencing self-doubt find it

challenging to spend time in silence; therefore, they are frequently wanting to be in the company of others and sometimes even dominating the conversation. However, when you feel confident, being alone can be a positive experience that is emotionally refreshing because you made a choice to have alone time. People who feel good about themselves can be involved in conversation without dominating; instead they are good listeners who don't interrupt with their opinion.

3. **Fear of Failure:** If you have self-doubt, you are afraid to take risk, and you tend to play it safe.

You do not stand up for what you believe in and you become paralyzed by fear and anxiety when you have challenging goals to accomplish. What you have to understand is failure is feedback to do things differently the next time. People with high self-confidence are not afraid to take risk; they believe in themselves and they make constructive adjustments to change and do things differently in the event of failure.

4. **False Sense of Humor:** When you have low self-confidence, you are prone to use joking as a mechanism to cope with your feeling of being insecure. We all need to have a sense of humor

because laughter is the best medicine. However, you must know your boundaries; anything done in excess is unhealthy. As you become secure and raise your level of confidence, you develop boundaries and your jokes or humor become more appropriate.

5. **Inability to give Yourself Credit:** If you grew up in an environment where you were told you should not have a "big head" or you were made to feel you were never good enough regardless of how hard you work; and you were told that you should not question what your parents said. You most likely grew up down playing your

accomplishments. In order to overcome this feeling of inadequacy and not good enough syndrome, you have to believe in yourself, even if it seems no one else believes in you. Even though deep down you know you are capable of accomplishing anything; the self-doubt keeps you from giving yourself credit.

6. **Indecisiveness**: Most adults, who have been raised in a home with at least one or both parents being narcissistic, tend to grow up with the inability to give themselves credit or they are plagued by self-doubt. They entertain negative self-talk and question their abilities.

These children are raised to serve their parents rather than the parents instilling in them the ability to become self-confident and independent thinkers. They grow into adults who are indecisive and tend to need validation from others or their parent because self-doubt continues to plague them into adulthood. While most people may experience some self-doubt from time to time, adults who were raised by

> *Do not allow yourself to shrink in the presence of others so they can avoid feeling insecure.*

narcissist's parents have an innate ability to question themselves because they were programmed in that way. It will take re-learning to be in control of your thoughts and feelings. You have to discipline your thoughts and know it is alright to give yourself credit for accomplishments without feeling you are bragging. Let your light shine from within as you exude a high sense of confidence, because you were created to be a light to the world, so SHINE!

Chapter 5

ARE YOU LIVING LIFE BY DEFAULT?

lived life by default for a long time, being unaware of it. My confidence was low and I did not feel good about myself. The bad thing is no one knew. I was doing all that I needed to do, but deep down, I was afraid and did not feel that I was good enough.

I had gone through a divorce, and I remembered the last words I heard from my ex-husband, "You will

> *When you spend time thinking about what you want and concentrate on being grateful and appreciative, you vibrate at a much higher frequency.*

never make it without me!" I actually started to believe it. I felt unfulfilled and my children were all that I lived for. I was unhappy with my job; even though I was paid well. I was not functioning in my purpose. I had great friends and a strong family support system, but deep down, I knew something was missing. It was just not the life I wanted for myself. I had a rumble in my belly and I needed to bring it out and turn it into a roar, and be the voice for those women who have no voice.

You may ask what it means to live life by default. Well, let's look at this. Let's take for instance your smart phone: when you look at the ringtones you have the ability to select a ringtone of your choice or you can select the default ringtone that the company chose for you. Just like the default ringtone on a phone, you are settling for what others have given or chosen for you. And no initiative, on your part, has been made to make a choice that will be in your best interest; to live life according to your plan. However, the key here is to know what you want.

When you spend time thinking about what you want and concentrate on being grateful and appreciative, you will operate at a much higher frequency of knowing; you are in a state of allowing; aligned with the essence of your goals.

The moment I made this mindset shift and began focusing on what *I wanted;* and changed the way *I looked at things*, things actually began to shift in my life. I got a different perspective, and I began attracting what I wanted. What happened? I began to create *my reality* and not someone else's reality.

I understood how to love unconditionally, because I had learned to love myself. Self-love can sometimes be equated to being egotistic or even narcissistic. Please, don't confuse loving yourself as a selfish act.

When I first started this journey of knowing my real self-worth, I was in a place where I was not owning or celebrating my achievements. I feared that others thought I was placing myself above them. After I received my PhD, it took me a while to give myself permission to own and celebrate my accomplishments. I thought I was being humble, but what I later realized, I was actually in self-denial. I was lessening my presence when I was among other people. I did not want to come across arrogant or

> *I learned that I deserved to lead a fulfilling life of love, abundance, joy and happiness; without shrinking back and playing small*

seemingly exaggerating my qualification, talents and abilities. In essence, I WAS DECEIVING MYSELF AS A RESULT OF INSECURITY.

So I had to find the middle ground and learn to value myself. Also, I strengthened my relationship with Jesus, my Lord and Savior. I learned I was made in *His image* and *His likeness* with my unique thumb print. In others words, I WAS ROYALTY because I AM a child of the most high God; the King of Kings. I realized I was fearfully and wonderfully made in God's image and likeness.

I had to come to the understanding that I had value and my talents, gifts and abilities they were unique to me, and no one has my thumb print. That increased my self-worth and it changed the map of my reality. MY STORY HAD CHANGED!

Therefore, I was able to bring balance to my life. I began surrounding myself with people who understood and appreciated my journey, people who had similar missions. Eventually, I finally felt comfortable in my own skin and this is when I realized I had a lot to contribute to society.

I believed I was born to empower and inspire other women. My talent was given to me to help others achieve their own outcome. I realized, like Esther in the Bible, *I am called for such a time as this.* So I have learned to pause and celebrate my wins, big or small and most importantly, be grateful. I encourage you to do the same, Say thank you often and celebrate your successes.

This is what enabled me to believe that I had the capability to do the best with what I was given. I learned that I deserved to lead a fulfilling life of love, abundance, joy and happiness; without shrinking back and playing small. I can now, unapologetically, stand in my power and be my authentic self, doing what I love - - celebrating my success and being grateful every step of the way. Just   know YOU can, too....

Chapter 6

LIVING IN THE MOMENT

Life can be brutal as we get caught up in the daily stressors. We all sometimes forget how to stop and "smell the roses." We forget how to laugh out loud and enjoy the moment. We are so busy at times, trying to be everything to everyone else this is especially true for women. This is what I call the "Superwoman Syndrome." We spend a great amount of time taking care and nurturing others that we forget how to be there for ourselves. Have you tried going to dinner or breakfast alone just enjoying your own company? For some women this will take a lot of courage, but it will help to build your self-confidence. Learn to enjoy your own company and feel good about it. I coached a client who did not feel good about herself. One of her assignments was to go to the movies or go to dinner alone. At first, she was petrified! Finally, she gathered up enough courage to go. She later called me and told me how empowered she felt. All it took was the will for her to say, "I can do this!"

> *"Your time is limited on this earth, so don't waste it on someone else's life."*
>
> *-Steve Jobs*

We all must learn how to celebrate what is going right in our lives, and learn from what may be going wrong. Most importantly, be in a state of gratitude, even if it is for that moment. Look for the good in every situation—good or bad—and ask yourself, "What was the lesson learned." Make it a habit of pausing during the day to say, "Thank you."

Every morning or every night, list five things you are grateful for. It could be your family, employment, your business, good health, your home, your car, food, clothing, nature, being able to see a beautiful sunset or perhaps, just for being alive.

When you begin to live in the moment—and in a state of awareness—it relieves stress, increases happiness and it helps to make life worth living. As you begin to practice being in a state of awareness, you will find that spending time with yourself is enjoyable. It is enjoyable because you chose to be alone and you had an opportunity to pay attention to your thoughts. Remember: thoughts become things, so you want to be aware of what you are thinking.

There is an internal dialogue going on in your head. Like board members in a company or church, those board members in your psyche speak to you. In most instances, they are likely to instill some fear. Remember **F.E.A.R.** is **F**ALSE **E**VIDENCE **A**PPEARING **R**EAL. It can also be stated as **F**orget **E**verything **A**nd **R**un or **F**ace **E**verything **A**nd **R**ise. You have a choice as to how you want to handle this thing called FEAR. You have to learn to take control of the board members and/or self-talk to quiet those voices. I have found that using affirmations help to counteract those negative voices. Say out loud.

I am exactly where I need to be at this present moment. My mind is at peace, this moment is exactly as it should be.

Also, we must stop worrying about what others think of us or what you perceive they are saying. These things are a part of *their* mental maps and *their* realities. Instead, focus on your own reality. We have to learn to create our own world and not allow anyone else to create it for us. Steve Jobs said, *"Your time is limited on this earth, so don't waste it on someone else's life."* We have the tendency to not pay attention to signals we receive from our bodies. We do this because we were trained to rely on our intellects and our own minds. Therefore, we are totally unaware of the signals our brain is sending to our bodies.

What we have to do is listen to our bodies. Perhaps your body is telling you to get up from your desk and walk around. Perhaps, it is telling you to drink some water or go outside and enjoy the sunlight? Could it be telling you to smile? Could it be telling you to relax or breathe deeply? Listening to your body can help you in knowing how to cultivate having better health, balance, and how to have access to more happiness.

When you are carrying around emotional baggage, it makes you toxic, whereby your body becomes poison. If you continue in this toxic state for a protracted amount of time, then eventually, you will find your organs beginning to rebel. They will attempt to rid themselves of all the toxicity from your past. If you are not cognitive of these moments, your body and mind could reject this cleansing by refusing to detoxify your spirit. When this happens, your spirit grieves, and your mind and body suffers because they are now being held "captive" by the excess garbage. This is especially true when we are dealing with un-forgiveness, resentment and bitterness.

Un-forgiveness is like a cancer; it eats away at you. When you hold on to un-forgiveness, resentment and bitterness, it is as if you are the one drinking the poison while expecting the other person to die. But the truth of the matter is you are the one who is tightly wound up when you have an unforgiving heart. And meanwhile, the person you are upset with is going about enjoying life; totally unaware that you are harboring resentment towards them.

Your lifestyle is connected to your belief system that is connected to your heart. You should evaluate your heart daily to ensure that jealousy, greed, anger, bitterness and un-forgiveness are not present. When these selfish ambitions exist, there is disorder, chaos and conflict. So be aware of what you are sowing.

If you want peace, sow peace and not discord. When you begin to identify and become aware that the negative thoughts and feeling you are harboring actually create the current state you are experiencing—and when you are willing to let go of those negative things—you will begin to make a shift in your life. This is when a paradigm shift begins to take place. Until you let go of the past, you will never experience what it feels like to live from your higher, authentic self or be able to unlock your full potential. When you arrive at this place of feeling free *and* happy, your confidence level will begin to increase and you will begin to love yourself and open yourself up for others to love you.

Ask yourself, "Am I living in my purpose?" If you don't know, then ask God, or tap into infinite intelligence wait in silence, and the answer will come.

And so I tell you keep on asking and

you will receive what you ask for. Keep

on seeking, and you will find. Keep on

knocking, and the door will be opened

to you. Luke 11:9 (NLT)

When you are living in your purpose, you tend to feel more confident and life has more meaning. There is ease and flow to life, less worry and less resistance.

You look forward to waking up in the morning because

life takes on a new meaning.

Chapter 7

THE POWER OF
THE MIND

When the student is ready the teacher will appear. Always remember preparation will always be met with opportunity. You need to expand and elevate your mind if you are serious about improving or changing your situation. If you are seeking good success; you have to obtain knowledge. Reading is one way to do so;

therefore, I encourage you to invest in your mind and yourself.

You don't have to be the smartest person in your circle to obtain success. Napoleon Hill stated in his book, "Think and Grow Rich;" you need to also have specialize knowledge. Knowledge you can obtain through *Master Mind Groups*. Andrew Carnegie stated that he personally had no technical knowledge about the steel business that amassed him great fortunes. However, the specialized knowledge he required was obtained through the individuals of his Master Mind Group.

As you acquire this knowledge through reading and expanding the mind; I want you to keep in mind this knowledge will have no value unless it is organized and put to good use for a specific purpose or towards some worthy end. It is often said *knowledge is power*. Napoleon Hill explained knowledge is only potential power; it becomes power only when it is organized in definite plans of action.

As you continue on your pursuit of knowledge, don't lack ambition and also be prepared because you never know when you will meet opportunity. If you are working on something and it is not bringing adequate results, you may need to make shifts; sometimes you have to retool, upgrade your skills or even seek out new opportunities in order to yield the desired results or outcome. It may be wise to join a mastermind group or start your own. A word of caution be very careful who is in your group, you want to be certain they are of the same mindset. Don't allow negative energy to infiltrate your mastermind group it will disrupt the flow of the group. All you need is an idea; if you don't have all the knowledge required to make the idea a reality tap into the specialized knowledge of the mastermind. You can then leverage the completed product or service and finds ways to monetize it.

Form good habits of daily routines. Successful people have daily habits. Seek opportunities and embrace them without hesitation. *Remember, success and failure is largely results of **HABIT**.*

Tip: It is not the quantity of books that you read but the principles learned that you MASTER!

List of recommended reading:

- ❖ Secret of a Millionaire Mind

- ❖ Think and Grow Rich

- ❖ The Science of Getting Rich

- ❖ The Charge

- ❖ Law of Attraction

- ❖ The Hero's Journey

- ❖ From Trash Man to Cash Man

- ❖ Mindset

- ❖ The Speed of Trust

- ❖ Switch On Your Brain

- ❖ You Can Heal Your Life

- ❖ Mindsight

- ❖ Lean In

- ❖ Pray and Grow Richer

- ❖ Passing it on

This book of the law shall not depart from your mouth; but you shall meditate on it day and night, that you may observe to do according to all that is written in it. For then you will make your way prosperous and then you will have good success."

-- Joshua 1:8

I can do all things through Christ who strengthens me.

-Philippians 4:13

(NKJV)

Empower "U"

Chapter 8

POSITIVE SELF-TALK

Yogi Berra once said that ninety percent of the game is mental. While Yogi was referring to baseball, this thought also can be compared to our attitudes. Like the old adage, your attitude determines your altitude. It is true in every area of your life. Just as your thoughts determine your destiny!

A can-do attitude and a healthy dose of self-confidence are some of the greatest components to you succeeding in life. *Great things will always happen to those who persevere in life no matter what!* Truly, it is not the quantity, but it is the quality. You see, a small amount of positive reinforcement can go a long way in boosting your self-assurance. This is why we must learn how to talk "right" to ourselves when pressing in for change in our lives. Because self-talk that supports our goals will have a greater impact on boosting our overall self-image than the opinions of others.

You Are the Master of Your Fate:

Do you feel that your life is lacking in some area? If you're experiencing challenges romantically, professionally or in any other area of life, know that *you* are the key to changing it. However, instead of playing the blame game with yourself and feeling defeated, recognize today that your fate can change the moment you change your thoughts and what you are saying.

Yes, You Can Do It:

Are you plagued with self-doubt? Do you feel like you're not up to the challenges that life throws your way? If this is you, let me encourage you not to give up because your spirit is capable of achieving greatness when you exercise your willpower and back it up with positive, encouraging reinforcement.

> *When you believe that you can succeed, you'll feel more confident in taking the steps that are required to overcome the challenges you face.*

   If you believe that you can succeed and you put in the effort, you *will* succeed.

One of the problems with doubting your abilities is that it creates a self-fulfilling prophecy of failure. You think you're going to fail, so your mind sets out to reinforce that idea. Your detrimental *thoughts* lead to detrimental *actions* which produce detrimental results. However, this can work the other way, too. If you tell yourself that you can succeed, you can also create a self-fulfilling prophecy that supports your success.

Positive Reinforcement is Optimistic:

When you believe that you can succeed, you'll feel more confident in taking the steps that are required to overcome the challenges you face. With positive reinforcement, even failures become opportunities to learn and grow. *You can replace the voice in your head that causes you to fear with one that pushes you forward by focusing on the good within yourself.* Convince yourself that you're capable of greatness by replacing negative thoughts with more productive self-talk. Then, when you *do* achieve your goal or overcome that challenge, you'll have an additional dose of confidence that will spur you on to greater success.

Cue the Music!

For big challenges, support yourself as much as possible. In addition to speaking words of encouragement to yourself, consider playing some music to pump you up. Whether it's the theme to

Rocky, Europe's *The Final Countdown,* or Pharrell Williams' *Happy*—even some Soca by Machel Montano—music can boost your self-belief and ease your worries. Studies have proven that listening to music literally changes the structure of the brain and strengthens the brain. If you don't have an MP3 or CD player handy, hum your favorite songs while you prepare for whatever challenge you may be facing. Inspirational tunes help to motivate you to take on challenges with grace and ease.

I enjoy praising and worshipping. This helps me when I need a boost in confidence or want to shift my mood. Another shift for me is dancing to my soca music, listening to gospel songs or doing a Zumba workout. Find what works for you and use it to bring you joy.

Your mind plays a large part in determining the level of success you experience, so tell yourself that you *can* do it. Positive self-talk will increase your confidence in your own abilities. When you add drive and willpower to your positive talk, you can achieve anything you want in life!

Detoxing your Mind:

When you think of the word detox, you may have an image in your mind of ridding the body of toxic or unhealthy substances. If so, this is true. Basically, detoxification means cleaning the body to neutralize and transform or get rid of unwanted impurities or toxins. The detoxification process allows the body to function better as well as help your bodies become healthier. We can do the same with our minds.

When we speak of cleansing our minds, we can use a similar process. When our minds become clutter with the cares of this life and the misinformation that keeps us feeling defeated, we can apply the detoxification process to rid our minds of these unwanted irritants.

If you are constantly stressed out, being indecisive, unable to focus on your goals or think clearly; you might need to detoxify your mind so you can think clearly. This is a good exercise to reorganize your thoughts.

Get rid of Negative Emotions: One of the many negative emotions that you can eliminate during detoxification is anger. If anger is a regular part of your life, you need to commit now to rid your life of this debilitating emotion. If you don't get this emotion under control, whatever you obtain in life will be affected negatively by it. You need to deal with anger and rid yourself of it.

But there is another side to anger, I want to address. Sometimes people suppress their anger, which is not good either. It is said, for the most part, people suppress their anger; but the problem with this is that when they do express their anger, they explode, causing their bodies to become stressed or even sick. You see, there is nothing wrong with expressing anger every now and then, but being angry all the time is not a good behavior to foster. Effectively handling anger rather than hiding it, will benefit you in the long run and you will be healthier and happier.

Focus on Forgiveness: Forgiveness is another negative emotion that can be detrimental to your health. In order to be at peace with yourself, you must forgive those who have wronged or hurt you. When you refuse to forgive others, you are literally turning your control over to them. Once you come to the realization that forgiveness is **for you** and not letting someone get over, you will feel better about yourself. Harboring un-forgiveness can cause sickness in your body. It is like drinking poison and hoping the other person will die. Rid yourself of this negative emotion and learn to forgive, see it as a gift to yourself.

Write your Goals and Dreams: Writing things down gives you the ability to clear you mind for higher level thinking. As you write things down; it clears up your mind to think big, allows you to see greater possibility and reduces the chance of you being a victim of limiting beliefs. When you keep your goals and dreams visible, it helps you to stay motivated and committed, in addition to making you more likely to achieve them.

Open up to new Ideas: If you become too preoccupied with your old mindset, you can miss new opportunities. As well, by focusing only on survival, you can miss success. When you open yourself up to receive new ideas, you invite newness into your life. Therefore, do not allow fear to keep you captive by refusing to open up to new ideas. Yes, I know it feels safe to live in your comfort zone, but you will soon realize that this place of security will become stale for you. You can never stand out in the crowd being a part of the crowd. As you open up to new ideas, you invite more opportunities into your life.

Enjoy Life: When you detoxify you mind things that you have taken for granted in the past will take on a new meaning. When your mind is clear it brings about new beginnings. It is like having a fresh start and taking a walk in the park in the morning. Having your mind clear is like the freshness of the early morning air as you walk.

You can also take evening walks and enjoy a beautiful sunset to elicit the same response. Laugh often, smile more and learn to take deep breaths-- exhale slowly, and allow yourself to gain new perspective on life. Do what you love.

Remember, *you are your biggest asset and you are very important,* more than those things you clean routinely, and put a lot of emphasis on. Use these tips to detoxify your mind. Also, eliminate stress, worry, self-doubt and negative emotions from your life, so you can enjoy your new beginning.

Chapter 9

Expanding Your Mind and Discovering Your Core Values

An effective method of identifying your values is to imagine your future. First you want to take the time to assess your life and reflect on different areas of it. After you do this, ask yourself these questions. Where do you see yourself as you get older? What are the things that are most important to you? What do you hope to accomplish in life? Answering these questions will help you discover your values. For instance, if you picture yourself growing old while being close to your family and spending valuable time with your grandkids, then a strong sense of family is one of your core values. You can have many values in life; you just need to discover which ones are your highest priorities. That way, at the end of each day, you can feel confident that you're nurturing the most important parts of your life.

Core Values

There are certain values that most people feel are important. You might find that they're significant to you, too, as part of your core beliefs. You can be a positive influence on others when your core values are aligned with the life you live.

Discovering your Personal set of Values. One way to truly know yourself is to get in touch with your own set of values. It's easy to get distracted by others' ideals and claim that they're your own. Many people are pressured into this. However, it's vital that you have your *own* set of principles and morals, so you can stand firm in your beliefs.

Your Values are simply the things that are most important to your very core. It's the unwavering belief in what you stand for. When you know your values, you can live a happier life doing what's most important to you. All you really need to do in order to discover your values is find what makes you *truly* happy. Then ask yourself why those things bring you joy. The answers will lead you to your core values.

If you feel like your life has taken a wrong turn, you can figure it all out by thinking about your future. Are you helping your future self while walking down your current path? If the answer is no, perhaps it's time to think about taking a new path based on your core values. When you do, that path will most likely lead you to happiness!

Complete the exercise on the next page to determine your core values based on this list. However, you can create your own list. This is just an example.

Select 10 core values from the list, next select five from the 10 and finally select the top 3 from the 5.

Arts	Independence
Advancement and Promotion	Influence
Affection	Freedom
Achievement	Friendship
Change	Growth
Close relationships	Loyalty
Community	Wealth
Competence	Personal Development
Decisiveness	Status
Excellence	Independence

Beautiful Inside and Out: Is society forcing you to change your outer appearance? The media places so much emphasis on external beauty and physical appearance that people are forgetting about their inner beauty. When you work on developing and nurturing your inner beauty; it shows on the outside.

List what you Love about You: Write down things you love about yourself that are not physical in nature. Are you compassionate, reliable, sincere, helpful, dependable, loving and nurturing? Are you a great friend, loving mother and spouse; a good daughter/son; or an empathetic boss? When you write down these attributes, you will begin to love and

Whatever you focus on expands.

appreciate yourself more as you have tangible evidence of your inner beauty.

Avoid Negativity: Detach yourself from Gossip, criticism and negative comments about others. Engaging in unproductive communication like this is a sure way to block your blessings.

Whatever you focus on expands, if you are focusing your thoughts on negative talk about others that is what you will attract to yourself. Make it a habit to pay complements and say nice things about others. If someone's appearance is not appealing to you, put a positive spin on it, then find something good about that person's inner beauty to comment about, always look for the good in others.

Using these tips will help you to appreciate and cultivate you own inner beauty. Learn to bring out the best in others by focusing on their positive qualities from the inside out.

Like attracts like, when you project excellent inner qualities, you will attack likeminded people that you enjoy being around, and who also enjoy being around you. As you allow others to see your inner beauty by honoring the good in you and celebrating for the world to see; your confidence level will amaze you.

Being Authentic

What is it to be authentic? Authenticity is when you become vulnerable, open, honest, spontaneous, and sensitive. You claim your individuality. You find yourself in a state of flow and are in tune with your feelings.

Ask yourself, "Am I being me or a carbon copy of someone else?" You are authentically you when you become the best expression of your truth, your feelings and your impulses, and you do this in every moment.

When you are being you, there is no desire to be defensive. You speak truth and you don't feel threatened. Mary Morrissey said, "One of the attributes of being authentic is to honor your discontent, then be in a state of awareness to see the expansion of the discontent and what is the real issue."

It takes some work to become your authentic you, but once it is found there is no turning back. Once you are in that space, you genuinely feel comfortable in your skin. Your confidence level increases, you have a desire to help others, you feel secure and—most importantly—you are eager to live your life's purpose.

As you begin to be honest with yourself, life will get easier. What you will find is that you will be able to write your own story or script, while inadvertently creating your own world – your own reality. And hopefully, from this point on, you will continue to write your own life's script whereby you will star in your own movie as opposed to living your life by default or in someone's shadow. I encourage you to find your authentic self if you haven't already. Believe in yourself, go inward and feel your essence, and then allow the feeling to flow outwardly.

I challenge you to let your light shine forth; stand in your power and really love yourself. Just be the best YOU, you can be. Remember in the words of Henry Ford, "If you think you can or you can't either way you are right". The brain does not know whether it is truth or imagined.

I strongly encourage you to believe and keep thinking that you can do and be everything you desire, even if it seems impossible at the moment. Set your intentions, dream big dreams, set audacious goals, and then let it go. All you need to be concerned with is the 'Why' and the 'What.' Let God, the Universe, Spirit, Source—or whatever your higher power is—take care of the 'How.'

Chapter 10

APPRECIATION & GRATITUDE

Learning to appreciate the small things in life can be very meaningful. I encourage you to get a gratitude journal, and each morning, before you begin your day, list about five things you are grateful for. As you begin to list things, you will notice your attitude will begin to change. All you need to do is take a few moments, each day, and express gratitude to your higher power. For me this is God.

If you are not happy with the life you are creating, press the PAUSE button, and then press the reset button. You are writing your own script and starring in your own movie.

For you, it may be the Universe, Spirit or Source...whatever you determine your higher power to be. This can be done through prayers or an act of meditation. By being still and going within yourself to connect with your higher power, or simply say, "Thank you," for all the blessings you have received will be a tremendous blessing in your life. Also, remember to be appreciative of the people in your life who have made an impact on you and have contributed to your success and happiness.

When you show gratitude; it opens up a flood gate of blessings for you. It will begin to attract more things into your life. So remember to focus on the things you are grateful for.

Learn to have an attitude of gratitude. There are times you will awake and ask, *"Why I am here?" "What is my purpose?"* The answer is…Your purpose is to live a full life, to be creative, to be happy. To be the light you are; brightening someone else's day. What are doing? You are creating your reality moment by moment.

Suppose you're having a "bad" day. You can apply

the power of "PAUSE." If you are not happy with the life you are creating, press the PAUSE button, and then press the reset button. Remember, you are writing your own script and starring in your own movie. Therefore, if you are unhappy with the results, you can rewrite your script. Simply activate the power of PAUSE. It gives you an opportunity to reflect and put things into perspective before it gets too chaotic or out of control. You can then add some affirmations as you rewrite your script. What is important to note is most positive thoughts have very little lasting effect on the brain. Therefore, learning how to intensify your affirmation will allow your brain to take the thoughts more seriously.

There has been research that shows merely repeating a prayer or affirmation has no real effect on the brain. However, once you fully immerse yourself in the prayer or affirmation, the manner in which the brain responds can transform a person's life. Therefore, you want to add emotions and feelings to your affirmation. Another good practice to feel appreciated is to create a "Know your Strength Board." This is a concept that was shared by Mark Waldman a renowned Neuro-scientist.

First, write down all of your best qualities. Next, think about what others would add to your board. Finally, call up some colleagues and friends who know you well and ask them what your strengths are. Once you begin listing them; you will begin to feel so good and what you perceive to be weaknesses will no longer bother you.

This is for all the phenomenal women out there in this vast Universe.

"I'M A WOMAN

PHENOMENALLY.

PHENOMENAL WOMAN,

THAT'S ME"

– Dr. Maya Angelou

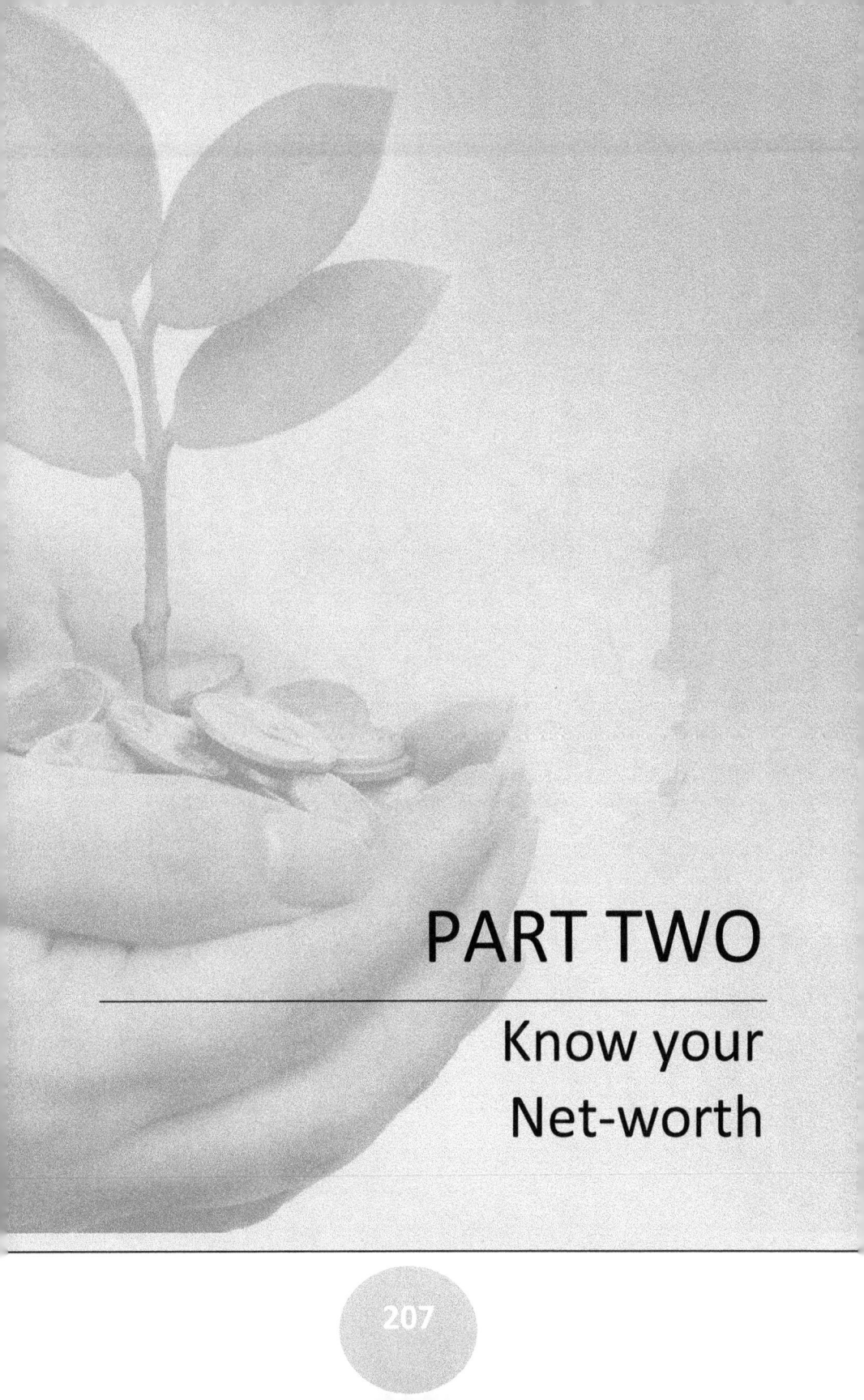

PART TWO

Know your
Net-worth

Chapter 11

WHAT IS YOUR RELATIONSHIP WITH MONEY?

I f you are having difficulties setting your fees for your business, it is evident that difficulties maybe showing up in other areas of your life. Ask yourself these questions: *What is your relationship with money? Do you owe money? Do you feel as if you do not deserve money? Are you afraid of money? Do you have issues with asking for what you want?* If people owe you money and have been reluctant in repaying, you should practice asking for the money that is owed to you. Get the courage to speak your truth even if it hurts sometimes. You have to learn to treat money well, nurture and value the money that you possess. Do not crumble money into your wallet or purse! Lay it out smoothly, in order, and lay it flat or fold it. Do this first and then place into your purse or wallet. Get in the habit of receiving compliments, money, or gifts from others. Learn to accept what is offered to you by others. I once heard Lisa Nichols say, "Money is a dignified conversation". You have to reprogram your mindset towards money and then *GET OUT OF YOUR OWN WAY!*

Beloved, I pray that you may prosper in all things and be in health, just as your soul prospers.

3 John 1:2. (NKJV)

It is great to earn lots of money, but it is most important to keep it and learn how to grow it. You must become a good money manager. Managing your money properly will also lead to financial freedom.

> *Your subconscious mind only responds and acts upon thoughts that are mixed with feelings or emotions and belief.*

Using affirmations is one way to reinforce new beliefs as this helps to build a positive money mindset. However, according to

Napoleon Hill, merely reading the words without adding emotions, feelings and faith is of no consequence. Your subconscious mind only responds and acts upon thoughts that are mixed with feelings or emotions and belief. You must have faith that you will receive what it is you desire.

Faith is the confidence that what we

hope for will actually happen;

it gives us assurance about things we

cannot see. Hebrew 11:1 (NLT)

Affirmations

An affirmation is a positive statement stated in the present tense; it helps to purify our thoughts and restructure the dynamics of our brains so that we truly begin to think nothing is impossible. The power in an affirmation is to repeat it several times a day. You can either think it to yourself or say it aloud. The key is to do it several times throughout the day.

Affirmations condition the mind and help you to develop a more positive perception. They can help undo negative beliefs that have been imbedded in your subconscious – negative messages we have taught ourselves or from others that have been instilled in us. In the words of Napoleon Hill, an incredible author,

"You are the master of your faith and the captain of your soul." In other words, you have the ability to decide whether or not something is going to happen for you. You can CREATE YOUR OWN REALITY based on your thoughts.

Repeat This Affirmation:

I accept with joy, pleasure and gratitude,

all compliments given to me. Money flows to me from

known and unknown sources. Money is everywhere

and I find it with great ease. People love giving me

money in exchange for my service.

Are you grateful for all that you already have? Gratitude increases abundance. Tell yourself that receiving money from your clients is a benefit to them for receiving your service. Charging your clients based on the value of your service, allows them to make a commitment to their own self-development and self-care. Paying you symbolizes how much they value investing in themselves and their well-being. Remember, PEOPLE PLACE MORE VALUE ON THINGS THEY PAY FOR.

Another way to look at or justify your fees—without feeling guilty—is to look at it from the MONEY IS ENERGY perspective. Building a good relationship between you and your client means having an equal flow of energy flowing between you both, it is reciprocity. You are giving this person a great deal of your undivided attention during sessions as well as spending valuable time with your client. In return they are giving you their money. Therefore, money creates a give-and-take relationship and a sharing of energy between you and your client. It allows both people to be energized as they

If you think "lack," then that is what you will "attract."

send energy back to you with money for your service rendered.

Most people grew up hearing "money is the root of all evil." However, it is the LOVE of money---and not money itself—that is the root of evil. Money is a tool or resource that we all need to be able to afford the things we desire; therefore, money should be enjoyed.

If you have negative beliefs about people who are wealthy and you see them as bad, then the probability of you becoming wealthy is very low. I encourage you to shift your money mindset and how you think about money. If you think "lack," then that is what you will "attract." The mind doesn't care! It will supply whatever you are thinking. The subconscious does not understand imagined or real. So, why not think "abundance" and "happiness," even if you don't currently have it. Remember: you must first CREATE IT IN YOUR MIND.

You have to remember that if you do not respect and value your self-worth, you will be doing yourself a disservice by under charging for your services. Even if you feel fearful, ask for the fees you deserve anyway. Giving into your fears about asking for the right value can hurt your business and ultimately your net-worth. If there is still some intimidations in asking; keep practicing and tell yourself, *"Asking for money is simply a muscle that needs flexing."* The more you exercise it, the better it feels, and the more confident you become about asking for what you are worth. One way to help boost your confidence about your service is to ask your clients for feedback. **What Are You Worth?**

List all the services your clients receive during a

session:

_____

_____

_____

_____

_____

_____

_____

_____

_____

_____

List feedback that you have received from clients:

_____

_____

_____

_____

_____

_____

_____

_____

_____

_____

_____

_____

Once you evaluate the services you offer, you will have a better understanding of exactly how valuable you are. Then change your thought process and accept that it is no longer an issue to charge for your service.

Your true self-worth is entirely up to you. Work on increasing it. Don't allow the pursuit of wealth be centered on only acquiring material possessions, because if you do, it can make you proud about your net-worth, but it won't necessarily increase your self-worth. It is great to acquire material things that you love; just don't let them define you as a person. Remember, self-worth trumps net-worth any day! But to have both and then add happiness along with faith... you would now have a total package.

I believe you are born with self-worth. Unfortunately, as you move through life, the comments, attitudes, criticism, high expectations from others and disappointments can wear down your self-worth. Self-worth is what enables you to believe in yourself; knowing you are capable of doing your best. This includes—but is not limited to—our talents, contributions to society, and the desire to lead a fulfilling life. It is, therefore, only natural to rebuild your self-esteem.

The Imposter Syndrome: Some people with the inability to accept or give themselves permission to claim their accomplishments regardless of the level of success they attain. When others praise them, they view their accomplishments as good luck or right timing. You have to liberate yourself from your own self-doubt and fear and believe in yourself. Do not allow yourself to shrink in the presence of others so they can avoid feeling insecure. You are unique and fearfully and wonderfully made with your own thumb print. So stand strong and confident, don't wait for anyone to sing your praises or validate you. Instead, give yourself permission to make choices without questioning or second guessing. You can do it!

Nothing or no one dictates that an insecure individual must feel insecure forever. *If you recognize these characteristics in yourself, know that you can take positive steps to overcome your insecurity and build a better self-image.*

Confidence and security in yourself and your abilities; will improve every aspect of your life by changing how you view yourself and the world around you. When you change the way you see things, things beginning to change.

Chapter 12

WOMEN AND MONEY

Are you growing your Net-Worth?

NET-WORTH = ASSETS - LIABILITIES

NET-WORTH IS WHAT IS OWNED MINUS WHAT IS

OWED

How are you navigating the current economic

climate?

Do you know your worth?

W e live in a world where everything around us almost says, "Buy me!" This is especially true with the commercials on television. They are especially extremely enticing so much so that this type of commercialism have created more consumers than producers. And while men spent a lot of money on their "toys", it is still women that do more stress shopping. Some call it retail therapy—which can become addictive if not properly managed, but whatever it is called, it can be detrimental if not addressed.

You see, the problem is people are spending more than they earn. Excessive debt is like having a ball and chain around your ankle.

As we prepare for retirement, working on becoming debt free should be a priority. Let me ask you this, do you know your net-worth?

Your net-worth is your total assets minus your total liabilities. Your assets are everything that you **own** and your liabilities are everything that you **owe**. List all your assets, and list all your liabilities. The difference between the two is your NET-WORTH.

It is a good practice to track your daily expenses. You will be surprised to see how much you are spending on things like coffee, lunch, shopping, and eating out. By tracking your expenses, you can determine areas where you can reduce your spending.

According to a report by Allianz, of the 2,200 women polled between the ages 25-75, 50% were fearful of not being financially independent.

Prepare a debt and spending analysis, you will be able to identify your pain points. For a variety of reasons, more and more women are becoming the sole breadwinner for their households. This has resulted in women being afraid of losing their financial independence.

According to a report by Allianz, of the 2,200 women polled between the ages 25-75, 50% were fearful of not being financially independent, of which 60% were the primary breadwinners. This statistic is even more complicated when we add the fact that women tend to live longer than men.

The question is, how well poised are YOU for retirement? People are living longer because of healthier lifestyles. As a result, we have more centurions (people who are 100 years and older) than ever. This means more money is required to maintain a certain standard of lifestyle, all the way through retirement.

Some tough questions need to be asked. Questions like: *"When will I be able to retire?"* *"Will I be able to retire peacefully?"* *"Will I be able to financially maintain my lifestyle throughout my retirement?"* *"Will I be able to travel and do the things I planned to do after retirement?"*

The stock market crashed in 2008, and it decimated the retirement savings of many baby boomers. Because of this, many feel the need to stay in the workforce. Some are still working because they are very active and have either changed careers and are now doing what they love. Some have even started their own businesses. If you were one of the individuals who lost a great deal of money during the market crash, you might have to play catch-up in order to be able to retire and feel financially secure.

Protecting Your Family and Yourself

If you have beneficiaries, I suggest you—at least—secure a good life insurance policy. If you don't have beneficiaries, it may not be necessary. Another thing you should consider is who you will select to become your caretaker should you become sick or you need assistance. This is especially important as you get older. Some younger women may not think Long Term Care

Insurance is needed, but I suggest that you do not overlook this step. Failure to pursue this can result in extreme health care cost. As we get older, the likelihood of a long term or extended illness greatly increases.

If you find yourself with excessive debt, focus on paying it down. You do not want to leave your family with excessive debt burdens, so plan well. A great way of combating debt is by creating several streams of income. You will be in a better financial position to sustain yourself throughout your retirement.

Chapter 13

ESTATE AND LEGACY PLANNING

D o you have a will, a living will, a health care Power of Attorney, and a general Power of Attorney? Have you considered setting up a Trust for your special needs children? If not, you need to speak with your attorney or financial advisor.

A Power of Attorney is a document that allows a person (known as the "Principal") to give permission to another individual to handle her or his affairs if she or he is unable to do so, or is unavailable.

A living will—also known as an advance directive—is a legal document created by a "declarant" (the person creating the living will) in order to make known the wishes of declarant in the event of a prolonged illness. This can only be in effect if the person ("declarant") becomes incapacitated.

A health care Power of Attorney gives the designated agent or individual the authority to make health care decisions. In the event that the principal becomes mentally incompetent or unconscious and unable to make decisions, the appointed agent can make medical decisions for him or her.

If something were to happen to you as a stay at home mother who has special needs children, who will be there to protect the dependent child? Do you have a Special Needs Trust? Once the Trust is set up, be sure that it is properly funded with Life Insurance. This will help to financially provide for the dependent child in the loss of the parent. The money in the Trust will help to ensure the necessary resources will be there for your loved ones, and to help the child to continue living a comfortable life.

There are a great amount of single women with large sums of wealth. Estate planning for a single individual looks very different from that of a married couple. Some of the planning strategies to protect one's estate from estate taxes are not available for a single individual. To avoid being bombarded by excessive estate taxes, wealthy single individuals should implement proper planning with their tax attorney and financial advisor.

Ensure your assets are protected from creditors or litigation. If you have concerns about the claims of future creditors, speak to your financial advisor or attorney about some asset protection strategies.

Have you reviewed your beneficiary designation and made any necessary changes lately? Does a trusted individual know where those documents are located? If you have children, and there is not a lot of wealth to go around, the best legacy is securing a Life Insurance Policy. This gives you guaranteed, tax free income as long as you keep the policy in force. Make it a point to leave a legacy if you have children. If you don't have your own children, you might have a favorite niece or nephew, or even a charity. The next generation does not have to struggle. Simply teach them how to be financially responsible.

Also instill good values in them then they will be able to create their own wealth, even in your absence. It is biblical that we should leave a legacy for our children and our children's children.

Perhaps you may know the story of J. C. Penny (the founder of the department store). After being in financial ruins when his business was hit by the great depression and the stock market crashed, he was able to rebound from his difficult times by borrowing from his Cash Value Life Insurance policy. By doing this, he was able to meet his business' day-to-day expenses. I suggest that you do not discount Whole Life Insurance. It is actually part of your assets because of the cash value that accumulates within the policy. If you don't have life insurance, you need to consider taking out a policy. The cash value will also increase your net-worth.

Savings and Retirement planning

Do you have an emergency savings account? You should build up a cushion of about 6 to 9 months of your monthly expenses. Pay yourself first by setting aside 10% of your income. Do this at the beginning of each month, or whenever you receive income. If 10% is too much start with 3 -5% and increase it as you go.

Make it a habit, eventually; you will be surprised to see how it will accumulate over time.

If you are a tither, pay your tithe to your church, or give something to your charity of choice. It is such a good practice to give. When you give, you position yourself to receive.

Make a list of all your savings and investment account balances. Include your savings, Certificate of Deposits (CDs), 401k or 403b accounts from your employer, and any other pension plans. Include stocks, bonds, mutual funds, real estate investments, cash value from your life insurance policy, annuities, gold or silver coins, and any other asset you may have. Once you have listed them all, indicate where they are located. Remember to keep that document with all your other important information; either in your safe at home or a safety deposit box at your local bank. Make sure someone you can trust knows where these documents are located. Diversify your portfolio. Some risky- growth funds, some fixed and guaranteed products is a good mix. If you are risk averse, you will want to allocate your funds to more income and fixed investment vehicles. Your portfolio diversification is contingent on your risk tolerance; it can be low, moderate or high.

Consult with your financial professional. Ensure that you have some liquidity. Liquidity is money that is in an account and can be readily available in cash, should an emergency occur. Do not have all of your money tied up in long term investments.

If you have all that I mentioned in order, congratulations! If you don't, press the reset button and begin putting things in place. You owe it to yourself to be financially secure. Money is a tool to be used to get the resources you need and to live a life free from debt burdens.

If you have been blessed to acquire a lot of wealth, some of this may not apply to you. Many rich people are so poor because the only thing they have is money. I hope you will not be a wealthy; yet, poor individual. A wealthy person might not have anyone to share her/his wealth with because of low self-worth or intolerable attitudes. This can result in loved ones separating themselves from the wealthy person. A rich person might be money wealthy, but lonely and unhappy within themselves. Do a self-analysis and do not allow wealth to cause you to become arrogant. Humility is truly a virtue.

Chapter 14

FINANCIAL SECURITY AND FINANCIAL SERENITY

A s of 2014, research has shown that there are about 9.1 million women-owned businesses which are generating in excess of 1.4 trillion in revenue. If you are a woman, ask yourself, what do your finances look like? Are you living a luxurious life? Are you living a comfortable life? Or, are you living a simple life where you just seem to be getting by? There are certain factors you need to be concern with as you examine your financial stability.

Are you prepared for the rising cost as a result of inflation (this means what cost $5 today will cost more than $5 in the future)? What about a sudden disability? Disability insurance replaces up to 60% of your wages (here in the United States). Will that be enough to live on? In the event of the

Life can be risky or things can happen suddenly. Therefore, being financially prepared is of extreme importance; not only to avoid leaving relatives with your debt burdens, but also to provide a legacy for the next generation.

sudden death of your spouse, what will your financial

position look like with the permanent loss of income; especially if he was the breadwinner?

Will you be financially secure to continue the same lifestyle? Have you considered Long Term Care? Women tend to live longer than men and may need to have someone care for them in their later years. Statistics have shown about 70 % of people turning 65 will need long term care at some point in their lives. Many baby boomers are now in the sandwich generation; taking care of elderly parents and helping to support their adult children.

If any or all of these things were to occur at any given point in your life, will there be enough financial assets to take care of you and or your family? Take some time and reevaluate your net-worth as well as your cash flow (money coming in versus what is going out).

Life can be risky or things can happen suddenly. Therefore, being financially prepared is of extreme importance; not only to avoid leaving relatives with your debt burdens, but also to provide a legacy for the next generation. Women and mothers are prone to do what is easy versus doing what is right. Don't be too over accommodating to your children by over-spending or being afraid to say "no." As women, we like to please everyone by doing what is easy. You have to learn to do what is right, and own the power to control your destiny.

In many marriages, the husband takes care of the family finances: paying the bills, handling the investment, saving for retirement and a college fund.

Some women don't want to deal with the finances because of their fear of numbers; some get analysis paralysis -- they just can't function. There is absolutely nothing to be afraid of! I encourage you to at least know what is happening. Be aware of the bank balances and what bills get paid at what time. Know the types of investments, the institutions where they are held, and the retirement accounts. Know the outstanding balance on the mortgage. Is there an equity loan on the house? Are there any outstanding personal loans? If yes, what is owed?

Please do not view this as taking over the financial control. It is much more about being fully aware; especially in the event of a sudden change (such as divorce, death, or separation) that leaves you in charge of handling the family finances. View it more as working collaboratively and less of wanting to take control.

Let us be realistic, we all want a happily ever after ending. However, it does not always work out that way. Therefore, in the event a woman is affected by one of the aforementioned life events, you should be financially and emotionally prepared to continue to live comfortably. Many women are forced to remain in relationships because they don't have the financial resources to live an independent life. You should never subject yourself to be treated poorly; this can only lead to living a life of depression and anxiety that leads to poor health. If you do not take care of you first, no one else will.

I am a believer that a woman should have a separate savings account in addition to the family joint account. Some may disagree with me, but you should have some funds for which you are in control of or have ready access to. What is amazing is despite the fact that a woman might be scared to manage the family finances, when she gets a handle on how to manage money, everything shifts in her world! Those around her are impacted in a positive manner. If she is a business owner, suddenly there is exponential growth in her business, and she begins to make life changing choices. This is what happens when a woman begins to own her worth.

Statistics on life expectancy have shown that women who will be turning 65 can expect to live (on average) until 85. One out of every four 65 year olds today will live past age 90. One out of every 10 will live past age 95. This data brings to light the importance of women having a solid retirement plan in place.

In today's uncertain economic climate, the responsibility of saving for retirement is shifting from the organizations to the individuals in the workforce. Therefore, having a plan in place is becoming a necessity in order to retire comfortably. Monitoring your portfolio regularly with your financial planner, or on your own, will help you to identify any shortfalls. It will allow you to be proactive in filling the gaps in your finances as you prepare for your retirement. Napoleon Hill said, "Knowledge is potential power, applying the knowledge and taking action is when it becomes powerful."

We, as women, have to understand that retirement is more like a journey than a destination. Your goal should be to grow your net-worth by providing an income that will support your desired life-style and standard of living during retirement. Women are living longer and retirement can last 30, 40 or even 50 years, depending on what age you retire. Therefore, if you are a young retiree and you don't feel you have sufficient income in your retirement portfolio, it is ok to work part-time or start a business to build some additional wealth.

It is understandable that parents want to save for their children's college education first. What you must realize is that it is easier for your child to get a loan and for you to co-sign. Oh, yes! I know you don't want your child to have any debt after college, and that is understandable. The fact is, if you need additional money for retirement *you* can't get a loan. I am not advocating that you give up on saving for college entirely. However, putting money aside for your retirement should be the top priority.

As you gain knowledge about handling your finances and building wealth, you need to take action in order to have a secure financial future. Sarah Ban Breathnach, author of Simple Abundance, stated, "We are zealous about pursuing financial security when what we really need is financial serenity." She stated that financial *security* is never having to worry about money again because you have accumulated all you'll ever need. "Financial *serenity* is never having to worry about money again because you've discovered the true Source. You have access to an inexhaustible, invisible storehouse of goods."

She further states that financial serenity starts when we accept as truth that, "Money is a state of mind and abundance is a state of belief." Most people equate wealth solely with money. In addition to money, wealth also includes love, inner peace, harmony, joy, happiness, good health and finding your bliss to name a few. Ask yourself, "How wealthy am I?"

I encourage you to live well, laugh often, love much and continually forgive. Live your life on purpose. Celebrate each day; it is a gift. Live in the moment. Show up for life. Be grateful. Be present. Have faith. Show appreciation. Dance like no one is watching. Recharge your energy often. Remember to say, "Thank you."

Learn to give; as you give, more will come back to you. Find your bliss. Keep money in motion. Be in a state of flow; being in a flow is a state of mind. What is important during this time is to remain focus on your goals. However, your happiness must not be tied to your goals; you simply have to enjoy the journey on your way to achieving success. As you know and value your self-worth, it becomes much easier to grow your net-worth.

Women are the catalyst that this world is seeking. Be an agent of change. Continue to break through the ceiling, push through barriers, and defy odds. Especially the odds that stack up against you and say you can't do it. Define what your inherent value is and do not allow others to do it for you. Know what you are

intrinsically worth. Shout from the mountain top; find

you voice. Free yourself from a mindset that is limiting.

Know you can... know that

you matter! Create a mindset

shift and change your limiting

beliefs about money. Know

that you can be, you can do,

and you can have anything

you desire. It begins with a

Thought.   Remember

> *Define what your inherent value is and do not allow others to do it for you. Know what you are intrinsically worth.*

everything is created twice:

first in thought and then in form. There is more than

enough wealth for everyone. Know your worth. You get

to determine how much you desire as you build your self-worth and grow your net-worth.

Just be HAPPY NOW!

Declaration of Faith

From Think and Grow Rich by Napoleon Hill

"Faith is the element, the chemical, which when mixed with prayer, gives one direct communication with "Infinite Intelligence." Faith is the element which transforms the ordinary vibration of thought, created by the finite mind of man, into the spiritual equivalent.

Faith is the only agency through which the cosmic force in "Infinite Intelligence" can be harnessed and used by man. Have Faith in Yourself; Faith in the Infinite. Faith is the "eternal elixir" which gives life, power, and action to the impulse of thought. Faith is the starting point of all 'miracles,' and all mysteries which cannot be analyzed by the rules of science! Faith is the only known antidote for failure."

Afterword

In this book the importance of having a positive mindset and being aware of your thoughts were addressed. When you are seeking change, one thing you must understand is you cannot use the same mindset that caused a problem in your life to find the solution. Therefore, you must be transformed by the renewing of your mind. There are 3C's to remember. If you want anything in life to **C**hange, you must make the **C**hoice to take the **C**hance in order to make it happen.

I encourage you to live a life of grace. Amazing grace! The most perfect life is a life lived in grace. The good thing about grace is that it is available to all; it meets us where we are. When you learn to give freely it is given under grace. Learn to desire grace for others. Connect with the grace of God and let it flow through you.

When you allow your deepest desires to come alive and flow from you, you open your heart to everything that is possible. My desire is that you have allowed your heart to be open while reading this book to awaken the qualities of your true self, and ultimately,

finding out who you really are and why you are here.

Become the change you want to see.

— Mahatma Gandhi.

Allow your presence to uplift and enlighten others

by becoming the spark that encourages others to grow,

live and prosper. Allow spiritual and material

abundance to radiate from you. As you continue along

this journey, like a child who is learning to walk; you

will fall down sometimes. The practice of falling down

will give you the resilience, the tenacity and

perseverance to get better, if you do not allow yourself to get bitter in life.

I am Dr. Ann M. Kappel and with the following, I want to EMPOWER "U" with words that you can repeat aloud.

I choose to love myself and to love others

I choose to renew my mind

I choose to be my authentic self

I choose to be happy

I choose success and abundance

I choose to love my life

I choose to change

I choose to live more deeply

I choose resilience over resentment

I choose Faith over fear

I choose to forgive

I choose to be motivated

I choose abundance over lack

I choose to be Empowered and stand in my Power!

I am grateful for the gift of Choice………

In Gratitude,
Dr. K.

CALL TO ACTION

Simple Exercises to a Mindset Shift

I am now free to love myself:

Learning to love yourself; who am I?

List 3-5 things you like about yourself

List 3-5 things you will forgive yourself for

List 2 people you will forgive. Call them or write a

letter; if they are deceased, shred or burn the

letter to bring closure.

List 3-5 things you will no longer criticize about your

self

List 1-3 things you want to change to improve your

life

Write out and repeat 7 times, "I love and accept myself, I am willing to change. I give myself permission to accept all possibilities into my life"

Self-Worth:

I free myself to be ME by creating my own Reality:

List 1-3 limiting beliefs you will release

List one challenge you will take that you were once

fearful of doing

List 1-3 things you desire to have that will change

your future

Write out the steps necessary to accomplish the things you desire to change. They must be specific, clear, concise and achievable.

(List the date you desire to have it, the amount - if it is money, the size if it is weight loss). List what you will give in return for what you desire? Keep it before you daily. As you think about it add emotions. See yourself already having it.

List your proudest accomplishment or win

List one of your most meaningful moments

List 1 talent or skill you possess

What is your passion?

Do you know your purpose? Go within and find what makes you happy when you do it. It may be as simple as making the lives of others better.

What is Your Purpose? Write it out.

Daily Visioning:

I open New doors to My life:

Value yourself on a scale of 1-10 and imagine what life will look like if you were a perfect "10" in any area of your life (finance, health, relationship, or spirituality). Now picture in your mind's eye the type of day you will have as a perfect "10" and see it unfolding for you. Practice this before you start your day.

Know your "*WHY***"**

(*The purpose, belief or cause that inspires you to do what you do).*

People are so much in the habit of asking **HOW** can I make this happen for me? When you have a dream yet to be fulfilled; what you should ask is: **WHY** do I want this? I believe two of the most important days in a person's life is the day he/she was born and the day you discover **WHY** you were born.

Steps to your WHY:

Get clear on your WHY

Become emotionally involved with your WHY

Once you are clear and emotionally involved, ideas, the right people, resources and opportunities will begin to show up for you. Ultimately your dreams will become realities.

This only happens when you are clear about your WHY.

My Why is…….

As I move into the winning circle, I am living a life of integrity, authenticity and significance. Everything I touch is a success. Every day in every way I am getting better, better, better. All is well in my world. Everything is working out for my highest good.

I greet each day with gratitude; with open arms I say, Thank You! Namaste.

Resources

The Bible – New King James Translation

The Bible – New Living Translation

The Bible – American Standard Version

Bernstein, A. BrainyQuote.

www.brainyquote.com/qotes/authors

Breathnach, S. (2009). *Simple abundance: a daybook of comfort and joy*. New York: Grand Central Publishing.

Hill, N. – (1937) Think and Grow Rich.

Morrissey, M., (2012) – Dream Builder Live

Myths of Retirement – http://iwc.tiaa-cref.org/private/participants/appmanager

Serendipity's guide to savings. Women Money Week.

www.savernot

aspendet.blogspot.com/

Workshop: Healing the daughters of Narcissistic

Mothers Virtual Workshop.

http://www.willieverbegoodenough.com/workshop-

overview-healing-the-daughters-of-narcissistic-

mothers

The state of women owned business.

http//:www.womenable.com/contentuserfee2014

US Census Bureau, Numbers, timing and duration of

marriage and divorce.

www.census.gov/pool/2011pubs/p70-125pdf.

Waldman, M. (2015) –

www.markrobertWaldman.com

About the Author

Dr. Ann Marie Kappel is purpose-driven and committed to empowering women to unapologetically live their best life now being authentically you. She believes women should stand in their power, be present, and show up for life. Dr. Kappel is the CEO of Alpha Consulting & Empowerment and the founder of Life Transformation & Connections, an organization for women *"where real change happens."* She masterfully integrates her extensive education as a Psychologist and Master Neuro Linguistic Practitioner and her many years of corporate experience to impact the lives of those she comes in contact with. Through her compassion, enthusiasm, and passion, she helps her clients develop a mind-set geared for success while identifying their life purpose by applying her transformational emotional wellness principles.

As an Executive Coach, she specializes in empowering leaders to strive to be their best selves, and achieve self-empowerment through personal growth and development. Dr. Kappel works with women coaching them to increase their net-worth and build their self-worth. She also coaches adolescents as early as age 13, who are not sure what they desire to pursue in college, feel stressed, have self-esteem or self-confidence issues and are seeking to improve their lives by way of personal growth and development.

Dr. Kappel is also an Adjunct Professor, Certified Score Business Mentor and Speaker. She coauthored Customer Service and Professionalism for Women and is the Author of her Signature Coaching Program, "The Empowered Woman: Twenty-One-Day Intensive" and her E-book, "The Empowered Woman."

Dr. Kappel will help you go within, unlock your genius and make a mindset shift in order to live life on purpose doing what you love.

For more information,

visit: www.drannkappel.com